Branches of Hope

The 9/11 Survivor Tree

Ann Magee

Illustrated by
Nicole Wong

Charlesbridge

Bright sun streamed down onto
busy New York City streets,
and the tree basked in
the warmth.

Until something unthinkable happened.
The sky roared and exploded.
Fire rained down, down, down.
Sidewalks rumbled.
Buildings crumbled.

Great black clouds billowed all around the tree.
Silence.
Then sirens wailed.
Time passed slowly.
Buried in darkness, the tree reached up,
    longing for the light.

Weeks later, a rescue worker spotted
something green among the ashes,
a sign of ongoing life.

The tree dug its roots deep into rich
    soil again.
Burned bark, like scars, covered the tree.
Winter came, and the tree slept.

Thousands of volunteers and city workers
    dug through debris—
day after day, month after month—at the
    tree's old home.
It was known as Ground Zero.
People all around the world lit candles
    and prayed for peace.

Season after season, the tree grew.
Each spring arrived with warm whispers
    and healing rain.
The tree breathed.
White starlike flowers adorned its
    branches again.

Leaders planned memorials for those
who lost their lives.
Families went to baseball games and
celebrated birthdays.
In summer the tree revealed a dense
canopy of leaves.
Birds built nests.
The tree grew taller, smooth bark
emerging from the rough.

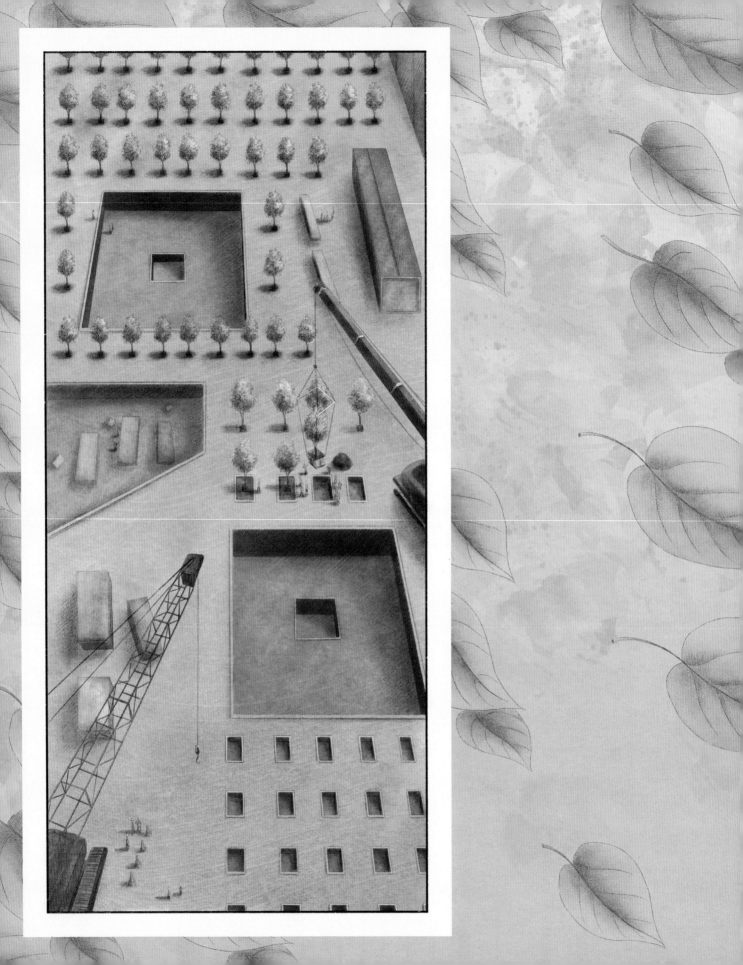

Workers constructed a museum and
   planted new trees in rows, like soldiers.
People hung American flags and marched
   in parades.
Cool autumn air brought other changes
   for the tree.
Colors of sunsets gilded the tree's leaves.
Bronze leaves, like flames, fell.

Children chased fireflies and attended
first days of school.
A decade had passed, and it was time
for the tree to go back home.

Bright sun streamed down onto busy
   New York City streets.
People stood shoulder to shoulder in
   the warmth, holding hands
and remembering.

Tears rained down, down, down.
Voices sang loud and strong.
The tree reached its branches toward the light . . .

. . . growing stronger every day.

More About the Survivor Tree's Journey

On September 11, 2001, terrorists attacked the United States by flying two airplanes into the World Trade Center's Twin Towers in New York City. Another plane hit the Pentagon just outside Washington, DC, and a fourth plane crashed into a field in Pennsylvania after passengers fought the hijackers. Investigators believe that plane's intended target was the White House.

More than three thousand people were killed that day, including more than four hundred police officers and firefighters. As rescuers sifted through the rubble at Ground Zero in the weeks following the attacks, one worker discovered the charred trunk and branches of a Callery pear tree, wounded but still alive. It was a lonely survivor of the collapsed buildings and fiery ash that had fallen.

When the Survivor Tree was discovered, burned and buried by the debris, few expected it to survive. It was transported to the Arthur Ross Nursery in the Bronx, where it was replanted and cared for. It beat the odds and regrew its lost limbs.

After ten years, the tree was replanted at its old home, where it stands today surrounded by a short fence next to the South Pool. Now the National September 11 Memorial & Museum's Survivor Tree Seedling Program provides seedlings for three cities each year that have experienced tragedy, honoring victims of natural disasters, school shootings, and terror attacks. These seedlings are cuttings from the Survivor Tree that have been rooted into rich soil, nurtured, and grown into small trees. Some recipient cities are Parkland, Florida; Orlando, Florida; Paris, France; Newtown, Connecticut; Madrid, Spain; Gulfport, Mississippi; and Boston, Massachusetts. Like the Survivor Tree, these trees represent remembrance, resilience, and hope.

NICOLE WONG AND DAUGHTER IN FRONT OF THE SURVIVOR TREE IN BOSTON. PHOTO CREDIT: DAN MEDEIROS

A Note from the Author

ANN MAGEE IN FRONT OF THE ORIGINAL SURVIVOR TREE IN NEW YORK CITY. PHOTO COURTESY OF THE AUTHOR

On September 11, 2001, I was preparing my three-year-old for her first day of preschool. Images of the towers falling flooded the TV screen before we left our house in New Jersey. Many young children, like my daughter and the girl in this story, knew nothing about the tragic event when it happened because their parents protected them. The skies were silent because all air travel was prohibited. It was a day of overwhelming sadness.

Much like the Survivor Tree, those of us who remember that day were witnesses to history. Years later, my children's homework assignments required them to interview me, as someone who remembered the events of that terrible day. Like the child in this story, my daughter was in middle school when the tree was replanted at Ground Zero. I found it incredibly difficult to relive the images and my feelings of that day. I wish I had known the hopeful story of the Survivor Tree then.

Hope lets the light in.

Selected Bibliography

"9/11 Attacks." History.com.

The Trees, directed by Scott Elliott (2016; El Segundo, CA: Gravitas Ventures).

National September 11 Memorial & Museum, www.911memorial.org.

"September 11, 2001: The Day That Shook America." *People*, special issue, September 24, 2001.

The Survivor Tree: A Story of Hope and Healing. New York: National September 11 Memorial & Museum, 2012.

For my children: Cassie, Grace, and Brendan.
May your hearts always be filled with light.—A. M.

For my daughter, Malley.—N. W.

Published by Charlesbridge
9 Galen Street
Watertown, MA 02472
(617) 926-0329 • www.charlesbridge.com

Library of Congress Cataloging-in-Publication Data
Names: Magee, Ann, author. | Wong, Nicole (Nicole E.), illustrator.
Title: Branches of hope: the 9/11 Survivor Tree / by Ann Magee; illustrated by Nicole Wong.
Description: Watertown, MA: Charlesbridge Publishing, [2021] | Includes bibliographical references. | Audience:
   Ages 4–7. | Audience: Grades K–1. | Summary: The journey of the Callery pear tree rescued from Ground Zero
   and replanted ten years later is presented alongside a wordless story following a girl and her firefighter uncle
   who is a 9/11 hero. Includes author's notes.
Identifiers: LCCN 2020017275 (print) | LCCN 2020017276 (ebook) | ISBN 9781623541323 (hardcover) | ISBN
   9781632899019 (ebook) Subjects: LCSH: September 11 Terrorist Attacks, 2001—Juvenile fiction. | CYAC:
   September 11 Terrorist Attacks, 2001—Fiction. | Trees—Fiction. | Uncles—Fiction. | Fire fighters—Fiction. |
   Resilience (Personality trait)—Fiction. | New York (N.Y.)—Fiction. Classification: LCC PZ7.1.M325 Br 2021
   (print) | LCC PZ7.1.M325 (ebook) | DDC [E]—dc23
LC record available at https://lccn.loc.gov/2020017275
LC ebook record available at https://lccn.loc.gov/2020017276

Printed in China
(hc) 10 9 8 7 6 5 4 3 2 1

Illustrations created digitally on the iPad using the Procreate app
Display type set in Active by Adam Ladd
Text type set in TodayBEF by Veronika Elsner, Guenther Flake GbR
Color separations by Colourscan Print Co Ltd Pte, Singapore
Printed by 1010 Printing International Limited, Huizhou,
   Guangdong, China
Production supervision by Jennifer Most Delaney
Designed by Diane M. Earley